MICHAEL PHELPS

BY MATT SCHEFF

SportsZone

An Imprint of Abdo Publishing
abdopublishing.com

abdopublishing.com

Printed in the United States of America, North Mankato, Minnesota
102016
012017

Cover Photo: Kyodo/AP Images
Interior Photos: Shopland/BPI/Rex Features/AP Images, 4-5; Martin Meissner/AP Images, 6-7; Jason DeCrow/Invision for Subway/AP Images, 8; Seth Poppel/Yearbook Library, 9; Gary Rothstein/Icon SMI/Newscom, 10-11; Andreas Altwein/picture-alliance/dpa/AP Images, 12-13; Mark J. Terrill/AP Images, 14, 18-19, 20; Altwein Andreas/picture-alliance/dpa/AP Images, 15; Itsuo Inouye/AP Images, 16-17; Heinz Kluetmeier /Sports Illustrated/Getty Images, 21; Al Bello/AP Images, 22-23; Lionel Hahn/Sipa USA/AP Images, 24-25; Lee Jin-man/AP Images, 26-27; Michael Kappeler/picture-alliance/dpa/AP Images, 28-29

Editor: Chrös McDougall
Series Designer: Jake Nordby

Publisher's Cataloging-in-Publication Data

Names: Scheff, Matt, author.
Title: Michael Phelps / by Matt Scheff.
Description: Minneapolis, MN : Abdo Publishing, 2017. | Series: Olympic stars | Includes bibliographical references and index.
Identifiers: LCCN 2016951817 | ISBN 9781680785616 (lib. bdg.) | ISBN 9781680785890 (ebook)
Subjects: LCSH: Phelps, Michael, 1985- --Juvenile literature. | Swimmers--United States--Biography--Juvenile literature. | Olympic athletes--United States--Biography--Juvenile literature. | Olympic Games (31st : 2016 : Rio de Janeiro, Brazil)
Classification: DDC 797.2/1092 [B]--dc23
LC record available at http://lccn.loc.gov/2016951817

CONTENTS

Michael Phelps races in the 200-meter butterfly at the 2016 Olympics.

BY A FINGERTIP

Michael Phelps stepped to the starting platform in Rio de Janeiro, Brazil. Some of swimming's biggest stars lined up alongside him. They prepared to race for the 2016 Olympic gold medal in the 200-meter butterfly.

Phelps dove into lane five. He was immediately behind leader Laszlo Cseh of Hungary at the first turn. That is when Phelps turned it on.

By the second turn, Phelps had taken a .43-second lead. That grew to .67 seconds at the third and final turn. But the other swimmers were not done yet. They raced to catch Phelps during the final 50 meters. Japan's Masato Sakai had nearly caught Phelps as they neared the finish.

Both swimmers took one last stroke and reached for the wall. Phelps got there first. But barely. It was the closest finish in the men's 200 butterfly in Olympic history. Phelps, at age 31, had proven once again why he is the best swimmer of all time.

Phelps surges into the lead in the 200 butterfly.

FAST FACT

Phelps had extra motivation to win the 200 butterfly. He had claimed the Olympic gold medal in the event in 2004 and 2008. But in 2012, he finished second.

EARLY LIFE

Michael Fred Phelps II was born on June 30, 1985, in Baltimore, Maryland. He grew up in nearby Towson, Maryland. Michael was the youngest of three children. He has two older sisters.

Michael had a lot of energy as a child. So at age 7 he followed his sisters into swimming, partly as a way to tire him out. Michael proved to be a natural. By age 10, he was setting records for his age group.

Michael poses with his sisters Whitney, *left*, and Hilary in 2012.

Michael as a child

As a teenager, Michael spent countless hours in the pool. At times, he swam almost 50 miles (80 km) per week. He grew to be 6 feet 4 inches tall. With long arms and legs, he seemed born to swim.

Michael kept getting better. In 2000, at age 15, he qualified for the US Olympic men's swimming team. That made him the youngest US male Olympic swimmer in 68 years. Michael competed in the 200-meter butterfly. He finished fifth.

Phelps dives into the pool at the 2002 US championships.

FAST FACT

At age 9, Michael was diagnosed with attention deficit hyperactivity disorder (ADHD).

Michael was just getting started. In 2001 he broke the world record for the 200-meter butterfly. He was still only 15 years old. That made him the youngest male swimmer to break a world record.

During the next three years, Michael became the sport's rising star. The teenager won six medals at the 2003 World Championships. Four of them were gold. Michael did not only win. He won big. He set five world records at the event.

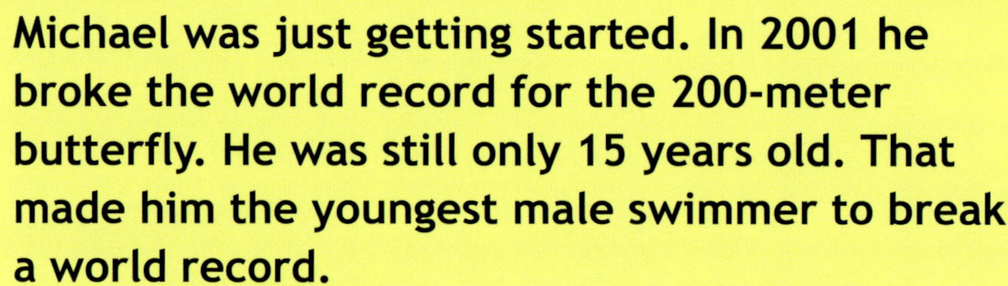

FAST FACT

Michael started as a butterfly specialist. But he soon became a force in other strokes, including freestyle and the backstroke.

Michael races the 200-meter butterfly at the 2003 World Championships.

OLYMPIC GLORY

Michael Phelps became an international star at the 2004 Olympics in Athens, Greece. His first event was the grueling 400-meter individual medley. Phelps not only won—he also set a world record. Then he just kept winning. Phelps earned eight medals (six gold and two bronze) at the Olympics. Only one athlete, swimmer Mark Spitz, had ever won more gold medals in one Olympics.

Phelps swims in the 200-meter freestyle at the 2004 Olympics.

Phelps shows off one of his 2004 Olympic gold medals.

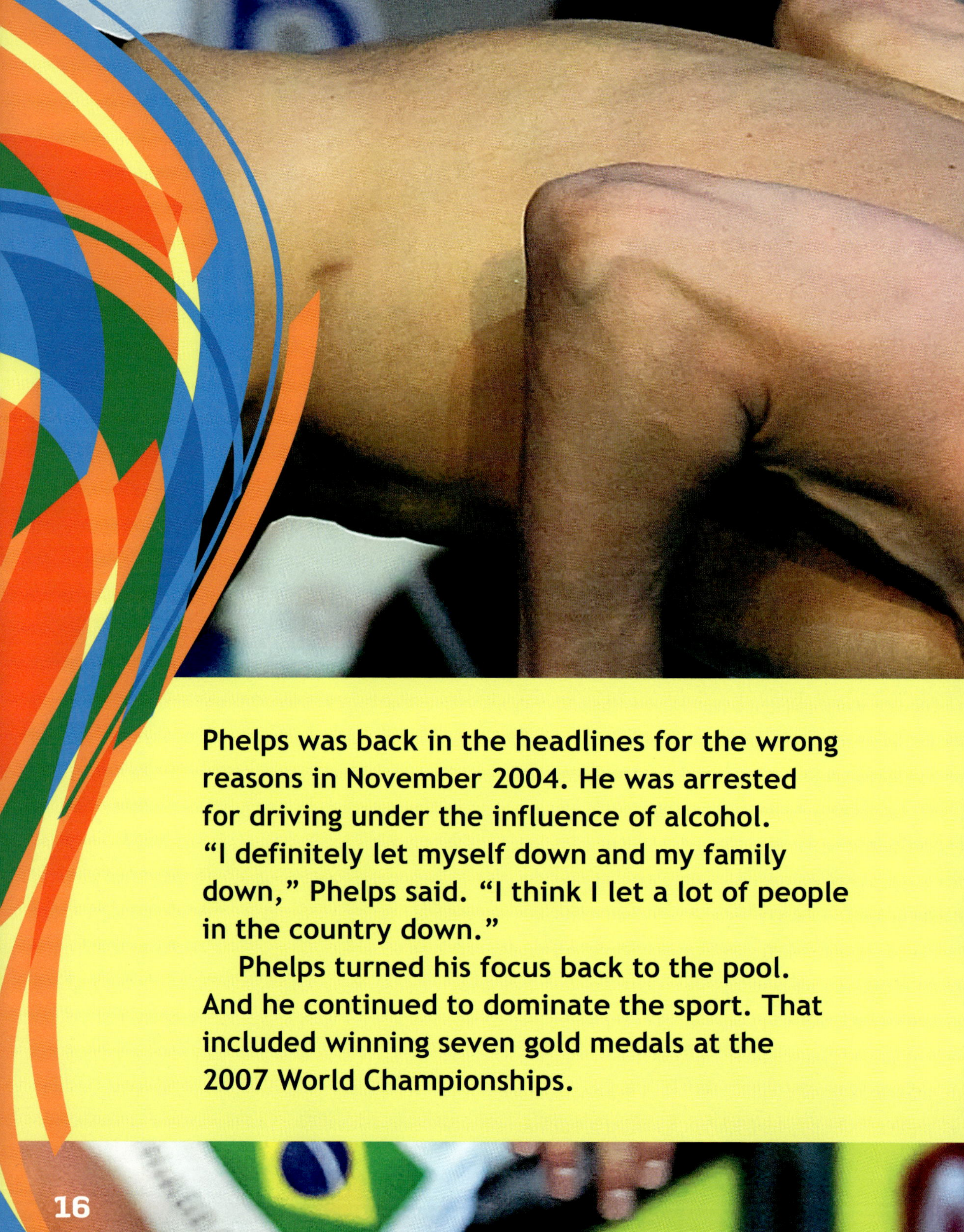

Phelps was back in the headlines for the wrong reasons in November 2004. He was arrested for driving under the influence of alcohol. "I definitely let myself down and my family down," Phelps said. "I think I let a lot of people in the country down."

Phelps turned his focus back to the pool. And he continued to dominate the sport. That included winning seven gold medals at the 2007 World Championships.

Phelps dives in to start a race at the 2007 World Championships.

FAST FACT

Phelps had hopes for eight gold medals at the 2007 World Championships. However, one of his relay teams was disqualified in the early rounds.

Phelps, *left*, and Milorad Čavić dive in to start the 100-meter butterfly final in the 2008 Olympics.

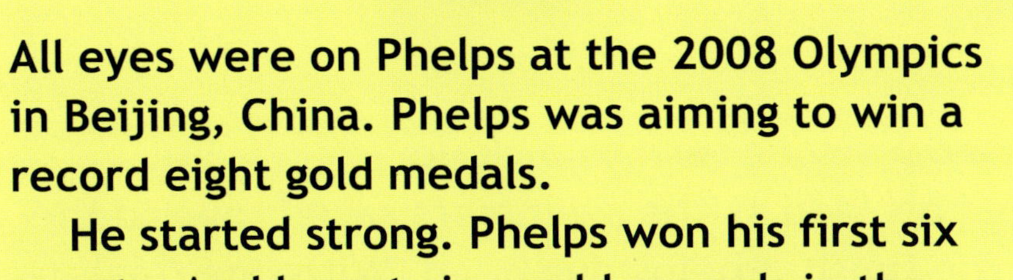

All eyes were on Phelps at the 2008 Olympics in Beijing, China. Phelps was aiming to win a record eight gold medals.

He started strong. Phelps won his first six events. And he set six world records in the process. But the seventh race proved to be his biggest challenge. Serbian star Milorad Čavić had a perfect start in the 100-meter butterfly. Čavić pulled ahead of Phelps and the rest of the field.

Phelps used a strong turn to pick up ground. But Čavić held his lead as the swimmers raced toward the wall for the finish. Phelps dug deep. With one final stroke, Phelps surged toward the wall. No one knew who had won. Everyone stared up at the scoreboard. Finally the results appeared. Phelps had won by one hundredth of a second!

"I am sort of in a dream world," Phelps said. With one more win, in the 4×100 medley relay, Phelps set the record with eight gold medals.

Čavić, *right*, eyes Phelps during the 100 butterfly.

Phelps, *top*, touches the wall just before Čavić.

FAST FACT

The only event in Beijing in which Phelps failed to set a world record was the 100-meter butterfly. But he still set an Olympic record.

FAST FACT

Phelps became the most decorated Olympian of all time in 2012. He left the Games with 22 total medals. The previous record was 18.

A TRUE LEGEND

Michael Phelps seemed to be on top of the world. Yet he was not happy. His personal struggles continued. In 2009 he was caught smoking marijuana. Phelps was suspended for three months. He lost sponsors, too. Phelps later admitted that he had not been taking his training seriously.

Phelps won four gold medals and two silvers at the 2012 Olympics. That would have been an amazing feat for most athletes. Yet for Phelps, it was a disappointment.

Phelps dives into the pool for a race at the 2012 Olympics.

Phelps retired from swimming after the 2012 Olympics. But 18 months later, he came back. Phelps was swimming well. But in 2014, he again was suspended. He had been arrested again for drinking and driving. It was time for a change. Phelps entered rehab. He got his personal life in order. In 2015 he announced his engagement to model Nicole Johnson. A year later, the couple had a son, Boomer. They married at a private ceremony soon after.

Phelps's mom, *left*, wife, *center*, and son, *right*, cheer him on at the 2016 Olympics.

The 2016 Olympics were Phelps's fifth. Fans were eager to watch him one more time. But few knew what to expect from him. After all, he was 31 years old. Some of his competitors were more than 10 years younger.

From the start, Phelps did not disappoint. First he helped the US men's 4×100-meter freestyle relay team win gold. Then he won the 200-meter butterfly and another relay. He finished his Olympic career with medals in each of his final three events, including two gold.

Phelps swims in the 4×100-meter medley relay at the 2016 Olympics.

FAST FACT

Leonidas of Rhodes won 12 Olympic titles in the ancient Olympics. In 2016 Phelps won his thirteenth individual title. He broke a record more than 2,000 years old!

Phelps has collected 28 Olympic medals, and 23 of them are gold. No one has won more medals or more gold medals. It is not hard to see why many consider him the greatest male swimmer in the history of the sport.

What does the future hold for Phelps? During the 2016 Olympic Games, he said he was done for good. If so, he would walk away from the sport as possibly the greatest Olympian in history. But many close to him are not sure whether he is done. After all, he said the same thing in 2012.

FAST FACT

Phelps has won 23 Olympic gold medals. That is more than some nations have won, including Mexico, India, and Argentina!

Phelps celebrates one of his gold medals at the 2016 Olympics.

TIMELINE

1985
Michael Fred Phelps II is born on June 30 in Baltimore, Maryland.

2000
Phelps qualifies for the US Olympic men's swimming team at age 15. He finishes fifth in the 200-meter butterfly.

2004
Phelps becomes a star by winning eight medals, including six gold, at the Olympics.

2008
Phelps sets an Olympic record with eight medals—all of them gold.

2009
Phelps is suspended from swimming for marijuana use.

2012
Phelps wins four gold medals at the Olympics then briefly retires from the sport.

2014
Phelps is suspended from US swimming after an arrest of driving under the influence.

2015
Phelps announces his engagement to model Nicole Johnson.

2016
Phelps's son, Boomer, is born. He and Nicole Johnson marry soon after.

2016
Phelps wins six medals, including five gold, at the 2016 Olympics.

GLOSSARY

backstroke
A swimming stroke in which the swimmer faces the sky and moves his or her arms like a windmill.

butterfly
A stroke swum on the chest, or breast, with both arms moving together and paired with a dolphin kick.

engagement
When two people decide to get married.

freestyle
A style of swimming in which swimmers can use any type of swimming stroke, although swimmers typically use the front crawl.

lane
A narrow section of the pool that a swimmer must stay in during a race.

medley
A race that combines multiple kinds of strokes.

platform
A block that a swimmer dives off at the beginning of a race.

rehab
Short for rehabilitation, a process by which a person works to overcome an addiction.

retire
To end one's career.

sponsor
A company that provides money to an athlete in return for that athlete's public support.

turn
The part of a race in which swimmers reverse direction, using one wall of the pool to push off and gain a burst of speed.

INDEX

About the Author

Matt Scheff is an artist and author living in Alaska. He enjoys mountain climbing, deep-sea fishing, and curling up with his two Siberian huskies to watch sports.